Drugs

Gail B. Stewart

KidHaven Press, an imprint of Gale Group, Inc.

10911 Technology Place, San Diego, CA 92127

Library of Congress Cataloging-in-Publication Data

Stewart, Gail B., 1949–
   Drugs / by Gail B. Stewart.
      p. cm. — (Understanding issues)
   Includes bibliographical references.
   Summary: Discusses the social pressures, family instability, health
risks, and treatments involved with drugs.
   ISBN 0-7377-0951-0 (hardback : alk. paper)
   1. Drug abuse—Juvenile literature. 2. Drug abuse—Treatment—
Juvenile literature. [1. Drug abuse.] I. Title. II. Series.

HV5809.5 .S835 2002
362.29—dc21

2001002964

Printed in the U.S.A.

Contents

Chapter One

Drugs Everywhere

Eddie is eleven. He doesn't remember what it was like before his mother was on drugs. She spends most of the family's money on them. Sometimes she sends Eddie down to get the drugs for her. He doesn't like to do that.

"I hate that she uses [drugs]," says Eddie. "But if she doesn't use, she acts real mad. She'll yell, she'll be hard to get along with. But if she's got some to smoke, she's different. She stays inside all day. She doesn't do anything. She and my aunt, that's all they do.

"I know it's bad for her. I told her that we talk about drugs in school. I said, 'Mama, you are doing just what they tell us *not* to do!' But she gets mad when I say that. She tells me not to have a smart mouth. She says I shouldn't worry, because she's going to stop using real soon."[1]

E and a Sick Baby

Shelley and her friends use a different drug. They go to parties where they take a pill they call "E," for

Drugs can affect a person's personality.

"ecstasy." Shelley says she enjoys the feeling she gets when she uses it. When she takes an **ecstasy** pill, she feels very happy. It is easy to talk to people—even people she doesn't know.

"That was the first thing I liked about E," she says. "I wasn't shy with anybody. Me and my friends used to take it on weekends. But now we even use it on school days."[2]

Another girl, who didn't want her name used, is worried. She has just had a baby—a little boy. But instead of being happy and proud, she is nervous. She had smoked a drug called **crack** when she was pregnant. In fact, she smoked too much.

"I couldn't get enough of it," she says, crying. "I knew it was bad, but it was hard to stop. I stopped, though. But I'm pretty sure I didn't stop in time. I think it hurt my baby. If he's a crack baby, it's my fault. And I know they'll take him away from me."[3]

"It's Very Troubling"

Such examples of drug abuse are not uncommon. Unfortunately, drug abuse is a very big worry in the United States. Parents have good reason to be worried, too. In 1996 the U.S. government found that children and teens were using drugs more than ever. In fact, the number of students in grades six through twelve using illegal drugs doubled between 1992 and 1996.

"It's very troubling," says one health worker. "We hate to see young kids trying these things. And it isn't always the same drugs. We are seeing lots of kids on ecstasy now. Five years ago, you didn't hear much about that one. And five years from now, there'll be a new one."[4]

Experts say young people are more at risk for getting sick. They enjoy taking chances. They don't think

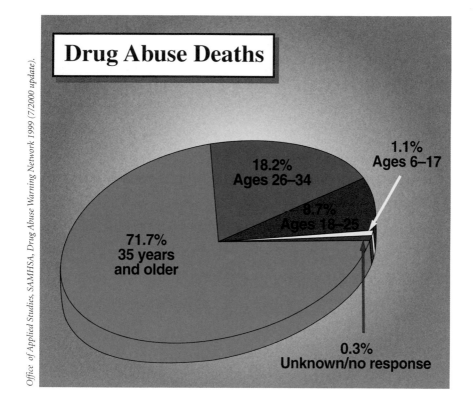

Office of Applied Studies, SAMHSA, Drug Abuse Warning Network 1999 (7/2000 update).

Drug Abuse Deaths

18.2%
Ages 26–34

1.1%
Ages 6–17

8.7%
Ages 18–25

71.7%
35 years
and older

0.3%
Unknown/no response

about the chance they might die from drugs. But teens *are* dying from drugs. In 1998, almost sixteen thousand teens died as a result of taking drugs. But the number of drug users keeps growing.

What Is Drug Abuse?

Drug abuse is sometimes a hard term to understand. A drug can be an illegal substance, such as **heroin** or crack. Using those drugs in any way is drug abuse. But other drugs are not illegal. It is possible to abuse legal drugs, too.

For instance, one girl abused pills she got from her doctor. She had been in a skiing accident two months before. The pills helped dull the pain. But even after her injury healed, she took the pills.

"I don't know," she says. "I liked how they made me feel. I finished the prescription, and I called his office. I lied to the nurse. I told her I still had pain. I really didn't."

She also says she was not following the instructions on the bottle. One pill every six hours was the correct dose. But she was taking them every three hours. After a while, she needed a pill every two hours.

"By the time I finished the second prescription, I was hooked," she admits. "My body needed those

Not all drug addicts abuse illegal drugs.

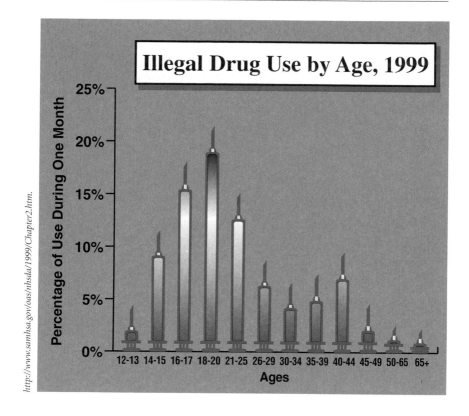

http://www.samhsa.gov/oas/nhsda/1999/Chapter2.htm.

pills. I would get fidgety and nervous without them. I knew I was in trouble then."[5]

Not Always Pills

There are other kinds of drug abuse. Some people use chemicals in ways they were not intended to be used. One example is to sniff the fumes of gasoline, paint thinner, or rubber cement. Inhaling these fumes causes a feeling much like being drunk. Such drugs are called **inhalants.**

"I know so many kids that are into that," says one seventeen-year-old. "It's called huffing, you know. I had a friend that was always high from markers. It's funny something like that can give off such powerful fumes. But it can. It seemed like she was high every day. And she wasn't buying anything—she was using art supplies!"[6]

Another girl tells a story about huffing. She had been caught abusing different drugs. When she went before the judge, he ordered her to a treatment center. She and other teens were watched carefully by nurses. No one could have drugs.

Sniffing inhalants is a form of drug abuse.

But this girl found a janitor's closet at the center. At night, she went in the closet when no one was looking. She sniffed the cleaning supplies. No one knew how she was getting high. Finally, she felt guilty, and went to one of the nurses. She told the nurse that there was an easy place to use drugs, right in the treatment center.

"She got this real funny look on her face, and said, 'Show me,'" says the girl. "So I took her over to the door of the cleaning closet. And I told her how there was all this stuff in there, but the door was never locked."[7]

From then on, says the teen, the closet was locked.

Why So Many?

Experts say it would be nice if it were that easy to stop all drug abuse—just lock them away in a closet. But that could never happen. There are too many kinds of drugs. There are also too many people who sell the drugs to other people.

Why do people take drugs? If they are so dangerous, it seems that people would stay away from them. What is it about drugs that makes them so tempting?

Chapter Two

Too Many Reasons

One girl was talking about her birthday coming up. She was excited, because she was turning sixteen. Someone asked her what was she looking forward to. Was it getting her driver's license? She shook her head no. She was looking forward to having a party where there would be lots of drugs.

"I want to get really, really high," she says. "I want lots of weed [**marijuana**] for presents. I've already talked to some of my friends. And they're all bringing weed."

She wanted to have the party out in the country. That way they wouldn't bother other people.

"But," she says happily, "I want to be so high, so drunk, that I don't even want to move."[8]

"I Tried It and I Didn't Like It"

Most people are not drug abusers. They would not understand why a teen would hope to use a lot of drugs on her birthday. One person who *would* understand is Rasheen. He has been using marijuana for nine years. He started when he was eleven. He says he started because his friends were using drugs.

Friends can be a powerful influence when it comes to taking drugs.

"I was hanging with kids older than me," he says. "They'd skip school, hang out at the park. One boy had a brother who was dealing. He'd get some weed off his brother, and we'd get high all day."

"The first time, I didn't really know about it. I tried it and didn't like it. It tasted bad; it made me cough. Made my eyes water. But I pretended to be high, because they were. I acted silly, talked funny. Everybody acted the same way, laughing. And after a couple of times, I got to liking it. I didn't have to be pretending."[9]

Shawn agrees that friends are a powerful influence.

"If your friends are doing something, you'll almost always try it," she says. "See, parents forget that. They don't remember what it was like being a kid. I think it's a trust thing. You trust your friends. Even if you know it is bad for you, you'll try it. I know that's why my brothers started smoking. You can't help but know it's bad for you these days. But all their friends were. So that's what they did."[10]

"He Said I Had to Learn"

Many drug abusers say that their families started them on drugs. Too many children live in homes where a parent abuses alcohol or other drugs.

By watching their parents, children are taught the cycle of drug abuse.

Many abusers use drugs or alcohol to escape.

"I've had parents who admit they use drugs," says one counselor. "They say, 'I have a drinking problem.' Or, 'I have a problem with **cocaine.**' A lot of them say, 'I'm going to stop smoking really soon.' But then they say, 'But if I ever catch my daughter doing that, she's in trouble!'"[11]

Parents who say things like that are missing something. They don't understand how closely their children watch them. By watching their parents, children learn lots of things—good and bad. And some parents even encourage their children to use drugs.

15

When the drugs wear off, reality can seem hopeless.

One boy says his father taught him to use marijuana. He says his father showed him how to roll a marijuana cigarette when he was seven years old.

"I smoked my first two joints with my dad when we were fishing one time," he says. "He said I had to learn to do it right. So he said he'd show me. And he did."[12]

Escape
Many drug abusers say that they need drugs to escape. They have lots of problems. When they use

drugs they can forget everything that is troubling them.

Carrie says she started using drugs when her parents separated. She worried all the time then. She didn't want them to get a divorce. And the fighting was awful.

"I got out of the house whenever I could," she says. "I hated being there. And this friend of mine, her father had some cocaine. She knew that he kept it in his bottom drawer, in a little gold box. And when I was there, I tried some. She showed me how.

"I really never thought of myself as a drug user. But that summer I used a lot. It made me feel so happy. But for just a little while. That was the bad part. Because when it wore off, my parents were still fighting."[13]

"I Was Out of Control"

Another boy says he began using **LSD**, or acid, as an escape. He was having trouble in school. He felt that his parents did not understand him. When a girlfriend showed him the special sugar cube, he was eager to try.

"There were a few drops of acid in the sugar cube," he says. "That's how they sold it. . . . Man, I was like tripping for four hours. I thought it was the coolest thing ever."

He admits that after using acid for a while, he was nervous. "I knew I was out of control," he says. "I was using it way too much. Even my friends were

Drugs come in many different forms.

worried. That was like all I lived for. Getting high, buying weed, or acid. That was my life."[14]

Many drug abusers say their lives are sad. Some are poor and have difficulty making ends meet. Others may have enough money, but they have no hope. They worry because they don't know how to solve their problems.

Addiction

One reason people keep taking drugs is addiction. That is when a person is unable to live without drugs. Scientists used to say there was only one type of addiction. It was physical. The person's body became used to the drug. After a while, the person would feel sick without the drug. When that happened, the person needed larger amounts. And then, even larger amounts.

Mary started using heroin with her daughter. She says that the heroin made them feel like nothing

Drug addiction can ruin a person physically and financially.

could ever make them sad. They would use a needle to inject the heroin.

"At first we didn't need much," she says. "We were spending maybe $20 a day, for both of us. But after a while, that little bit didn't do anything. It was nothing. My daughter thought the dealer cheated us. Maybe he sold us something that just looked like heroin. But no, it was heroin. But we just needed more of it to feel good. So we started spending more money. Instead of one packet, we'd buy two or three. By August, I think we were spending more than $200 a day on heroin."[15]

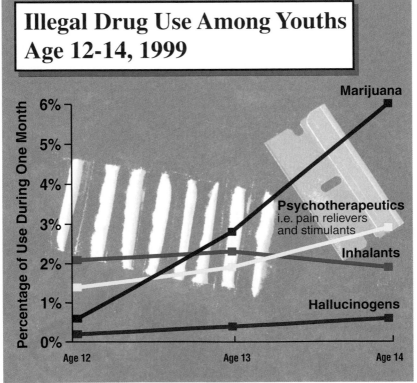

Illegal Drug Use Among Youths Age 12-14, 1999

http://www.samhsa.gov/oas/nhsda/1999/Chapter2.htm.

The Mind Can Get Addicted, Too

Scientists say there are other ways to be addicted. It isn't just physical. Some drug users are addicted to the feeling they get. Their bodies don't crave drugs, but their minds do.

One boy knows that he is addicted this way. "I'm a weed addict," he admits. "I know that some people say that weed isn't addictive. But that isn't right. You get addicted to the way you feel when you are smoking it."

He says that he doesn't like himself unless he is on drugs. "It's like when I'm high, I'm best," he says. "It's the way I feel the best. I'm on point. I understand things around me. I can do things."[16]

A Different Story

Drug abusers say their lives seem better when they are high. Their problems don't seem so bad. They feel smarter. They forget about things that make them sad.

But there is a different story about drugs. It is a story of people whose lives are ruined. These people commit crimes. They hurt their families and friends. This story is familiar to people who are trying to get away from drugs.

Chapter Three

A Bad Kind of Life

Martin and Rose have always lived in the west part of the city. They have a small home by the river. Their four children grew up in this house. There are many good memories in the neighborhood. Rose loved sitting outside on summer nights. She liked waving at the neighbors.

But lately, the area around their house is not so nice. There is more noise now, and more loud music. Teenagers are outside at night, and often gangs of them fight. Several of their neighbors have had break-ins. Last August there was a shooting, and three teenagers were hurt.

"My youngest son works for the police department," says Rose. "He says there is a lot of crack being sold here. Lots of people selling and buying, I guess. It makes us sad, thinking about how it was here not too long ago. We didn't know everybody, but we knew most people. Martin and I don't even sit outside in the evenings. It's too dangerous."[17]

Gang activity and drug dealing hurt many communities.

Lots of Victims

Drug abuse hurts many communities. As more people turn to drugs, more **dealers** come around. Often, dealers fight with one another over who gets what territory. And because dealers are often gang members, the fights are dangerous.

Luis, twelve, lives near a park on the south part of the city. He and his brothers and sisters love to be outside. But their mother won't let them. She knows there are gangs in the park. In fact, two weeks ago, there was a murder there. One dealer killed another. Luis complains that the drug dealers are ruining his life.

"It ticks me off," he says. "I don't take drugs. No one in my family does. But who gets to go to the park? Not us. Just the dealers, man. And the **dopers** [drug buyers]. That's so unfair. We get mad at my mom, but she's just trying to keep us safe. But I hate staying inside, especially on nice days."[18]

Drugs change a neighborhood in other ways. People who abuse drugs don't paint their houses. They don't cut their grass or plant flowers. Gradually, the neighborhood begins to look shabby. No one seems to care, and that hurts everyone.

"I Don't Remember Feeding Them"

People who abuse drugs often ignore something else—their children. One young mother has been addicted to crack for years. She knows it is bad for her. She knows that when she uses crack, she forgets

Drug addicts may forget to care for their children.

about her children. But it's hard for her to live
without it.

She says that four years ago, she was using a lot
of crack. She doesn't remember very much about
that time. Did she read to her children? Did she
play with them? She shakes her head sadly.

"Hey, I don't think I even picked them up when I was smoking," she says. "I don't remember feeding them. I might have, but I think someone else might have. My oldest was four. He had a lot of cereal then, I guess. Those were bad days."[19]

Other drug abusers say that nothing seems important when they use drugs. One woman said she would go for weeks without washing her hair. She never took a shower or brushed her teeth. All she cared about was getting more drugs.

Gradual Death

There are many ways drugs can hurt a user. Drugs can kill people. Sometimes they can cause a person's

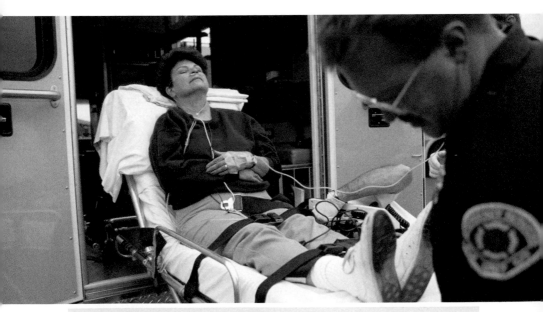

Drugs can physically harm or even kill a person.

heart to beat in an irregular way. Sometimes the drug can cause reactions in breathing or blood pressure. A person may die quickly of a heart attack, a stroke, or a seizure.

But deaths from drug use usually happen gradually. Damage to the lungs or the heart can take years to kill. People who use inhalants can develop liver problems. They get brain damage, too. Those things show up over time. Many drug users get HIV or **AIDS,** too. They get these viruses not from the drugs themselves, but the way they take the drugs.

Mary, who took heroin years ago, caught AIDS. She got it from using the same needle as a person with the virus. The needle had tiny amounts of the virus from the other person. When Mary used that needle to inject heroin, the virus entered her body.

She stopped taking heroin because she was tired of being a drug abuser. She wanted a fresh start. But she soon learned that it was too late for that. Using heroin had caused her to get a disease that will soon kill her.

"I wish I'd never started those drugs," says Mary, wiping her eyes with a tissue. "I'd give anything for that."[20]

"Death of the Spirit"
The death of a person is a sad thing. But people sometimes die before their bodies are actually dead. One drug counselor says that drug abusers often die like that.

"I call it a death of the spirit," says Curtis, who works with drug abusers. "Gradually the dreams go away. They don't hope any more. They don't laugh or plan things that are fun. They don't have a purpose. They're all about getting the next high, making the next buy.

"They do things they would never have done before. They steal, just for drug money. They sell drugs themselves, to make drug money. We've all heard the stories of the mothers who try to sell their own kids for drug money. That's death of the spirit."[21]

One Milwaukee teen knows about stealing. He and his brother stole bicycles and cars. They broke into houses looking for money. It was all to buy drugs.

"That was the thing," he says. "We were taking stupid risks. We'd break into houses when we weren't even sure if the people were gone. We knew we had to get money or we'd be messed up. That's all me and him were thinking about. We didn't want to be messed up, not having a [drug] score when we needed it."[22]

Violence and Drugs

Drug abusers say that they sometimes would feel desperate. They would worry about running short of drug money. Some say that they would do almost anything to get more.

"Doing anything means hurt somebody," says Curtis. "It means carry a gun, it means shoot some-

People sometimes turn to crime to get money for drugs.

one for their wallet. That's more of this spirit death. You know right from wrong. You never were a killer. But now here you are, with your gun. You have to say to yourself, 'What has happened to me?'"

One boy became dependent on marijuana. But one afternoon, he didn't have enough money to buy some. Even though he was usually shy, he took

Drugs can cause emotional harm.

Once dependent on drugs, some people will steal or deal drugs to buy more.

part in a violent crime. He helped a friend rob another boy at knifepoint. They wanted money to buy marijuana.

"I tell people in treatment to say their name out loud," says Curtis. "I say, 'You hear that name? Does that name mean anything to you? Does it stand for something good, or something no-good?' When drug abusers think about that, it scares them sometimes. It's scary when you forget who you really are."[23]

Chapter Four

Doing Something About It

Drug treatment centers, like the one where Curtis works, are a first step. But many drug users don't want to get treatment. They get nervous thinking about giving up drugs. How would they manage without marijuana, heroin, or crack?

Many people are in treatment because someone else made them go. For instance, fourteen-year-old Grace was brought to a treatment center by her father.

"I was taking **speed,**" she says. "And **crank,** which is like speed. I told my parents I was just drinking a lot of Mountain Dew. That has caffeine, and I told them I was just wired from that. But I passed out one night. I hit my head on the counter, and my dad knew something was really wrong."

Grace said the hospital knew she was abusing drugs. They took blood tests, and that's how they knew. The doctors told her parents she needed to be in a place that was locked. It wasn't just to keep Grace in. It was to keep drugs out, too.

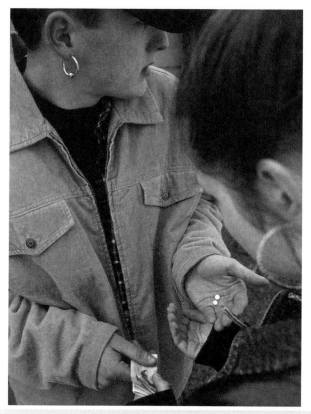

Learning why a person takes drugs can be the first step to his or her recovery.

"It took me eight months to get better," she says. "I'm at home now. I go to school half-days. I worry that I'll see my old friends that I did drugs with. I don't want to go back to using again."[24]

"The Talking Helps"

A lot of time in treatment is spent finding why the person took drugs in the first place. One boy says that "why did you do it?" was more important than "what did you do?"

Talking can help a person recover from drug addiction.

"Nobody really cared what you were on," he says. "But they wanted you to talk about why you were unhappy. You gotta work on what makes you feel unhappy or just bad, or whatever. If you can get to the cause, you won't have the drug problem."

He says that many kids don't like to talk. They sulk. Sometimes they stomp back to their rooms. But the counselors are patient. They know that a teen will talk when he or she is ready.

"The talking helps," he admits. "I figured out what was making me angry. That's why I was using drugs. I was angry at my mom and dad. Now I'm working to deal with that."[25]

Prevention

It isn't just drug abusers who are fighting the problem. Others are fighting it, too, in many different ways. For instance, state and federal government programs are changing. Billions of dollars have been spent trying to catch drug dealers and those who bring in drugs from other places. But now, more money is being spent on preventing drug abuse.

The government spends billions of dollars trying to catch drug dealers.

Antidrug programs can be very successful.

"There's no way to stop all the drugs that are coming in," says one man. "You see police checking people when they enter the country. They search luggage, they search your car. But very little is seized. Better to get rid of the market. If people didn't need drugs, they wouldn't buy them."[26]

Experts know that drug use usually starts early. Waiting until high school to educate people about the dangers of drugs is too late. Communities and schools are working together. They want to make sure children have fun things to do. They know that children who are busy and happy don't need drugs.

"We see so many kids who are idle," says one park worker. "They hang out in the park. They've got nothing going on, and that's a risk. But then somebody starts a cooking class, teaching kids to make brownies and snacks. And someone else starts a soccer league after school. And pretty soon, those kids aren't idle anymore."[27]

Hotlines and After-Care

Some towns have drug hotlines. These are numbers people can call if they think someone they know may need help. One boy called because he was worried about his brother's drug use. Another called because he wanted to get into treatment, but wasn't sure how.

Some communities help build better treatment centers. The newest ones are bright, cheerful places. They are not prisons, even though they keep doors locked. The best part is that they help even after the treatment is over. Former drug users like this program, called after-care. They feel better knowing that the staff is always willing to help.

"I'd been in treatment for six months," says one teen. "I knew it would be hard coming back home. My friends all use drugs. I worried about what I would do when I saw them. Would I slide back into it? But the staff at the center called. We got together a few times for dinner. We talked about how I was doing. I felt like they really wanted me to do well. And so far, I've been doing great!"[28]

Getting Tougher on Dealers

Some antidrug programs are very successful. One program is aimed at children who are at risk for using drugs. Program leaders took the children to a hospital. They visited the new babies, and saw some that wouldn't stop crying.

"It was horrible," says one girl. "I never seen a baby cry like that. First off, it was real little—a crack baby. It looked like it was half as big as it should have been. And it just kept crying and making these noises. I felt real bad. The nurses said this baby—he was two days old. And he was addicted to crack. That's why he was crying."[29]

Seeing what drug abuse can do is often scary and sad. One group visited a different part of the hospital where they met a drug dealer who was in a gang. He had been shot by another drug dealer.

"He wasn't going to walk ever again," says one boy in the group. "He used to be tough, but now he just sits in the chair. Can't move, can't do anything. They feed him, help him go to the bathroom. I never seen somebody young like that, so messed up. It could have been any dealer, you know?"[30]

Knowing More

It's so important for people to learn more about drug abuse. It is one of the most dangerous problems in

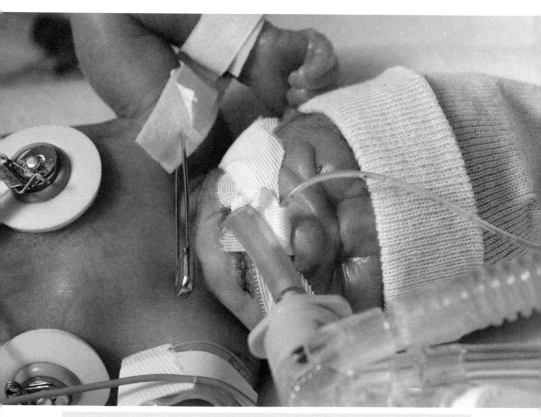

If a woman does drugs while pregnant, her baby can be born an addict.

Smarter, healthier choices come from learning as much as possible about drugs.

the United States today. Knowing how damaging drugs can be helps people make good decisions.

All children will make choices about drugs. Will I try smoking? Will I smoke marijuana, or drink beer? Is it okay to try ecstasy once? Learning as much as possible can lead to smarter, healthier choices. And that is good for everyone.

Notes

Chapter One: Drugs Everywhere

1. Personal interview, Eddie, Minneapolis, MN, March 19–20, 1999.
2. Telephone interview, Shelley, May 1, 2001.
3. Personal interview, (name withheld), Minneapolis, MN, August 1996.
4. Personal interview, Kara, St. Paul, MN, April 23, 1999.
5. Personal interview, (name withheld), Minneapolis, MN, October 1998.
6. Personal interview, (name withheld), Minneapolis, MN, March 1999.
7. Personal interview, (name withheld), Minneapolis, MN, October 1998.

Chapter Two: Too Many Reasons

8. Personal interview, (name withheld), Crystal, MN, November 1999.
9. Personal interview, Rasheen, St. Paul, MN, April 1999.
10. Personal interview, Shawn, Minneapolis, MN, August 1999.
11. Telephone interview, Lynne, April 30, 2001.
12. Personal interview, (name withheld), Minneapolis, MN, April 1998.
13. Telephone interview, Carrie, July 1, 1998.
14. Personal interview, (name withheld), November 7, 1999.

15. Personal interview, Mary, Minneapolis, MN, May 1995.
16. Telephone interview, (name withheld), April 1999.

Chapter Three: A Bad Kind of Life

17. Telephone interview, Rose, May 1, 2001.
18. Personal interview, Luis, Minneapolis, MN, August 11, 1997.
19. Personal interview, (name withheld), Minneapolis, MN, November 2, 1999.
20. Mary, May 1995.
21. Personal interview, Curtis, Eagan, MN, January 1998.
22. Telephone interview, (name withheld), March 12, 1998.
23. Curtis, January 1998.

Chapter Four: Doing Something About It

24. Personal interview, Grace, St. Louis Park, MN, April 2001.
25. Personal interview, (name withheld), Minneapolis, MN, November 2, 1999.
26. Telephone interview, Charlie, May 3, 2001.
27. Telephone interview, Dick, May 2, 2001.
28. Personal interview, (name withheld), Minneapolis, MN, October 1999.
29. Personal interview, (name withheld), St. Paul, MN, October 1999.
30. Personal interview, (name withheld), Richfield, MN, September 13, 1998.

Glossary

AIDS: A deadly disease that can spread by drug users sharing needles.

cocaine: A very powerful, addictive drug that speeds up the work of the body.

crack: A very powerful form of cocaine.

crank: A form of speed that can be smoked.

dealers: Those who sell drugs to drug users.

dopers: A slang term for a drug user.

ecstasy: A drug that gives the user a short-lived feeling of happiness. Popular with some teens and young adults, it is also called "E."

heroin: A very powerful, addictive drug. It can be taken through the skin with a needle, by smoking, or sniffing through the nose.

inhalants: Chemicals that have strong fumes. Some drug abusers sniff the chemicals, which produce a "high."

LSD: Also known as "acid," LSD causes users to hallucinate, or see things that aren't there.

marijuana: Known as "pot," "weed," and other names, marijuana is usually smoked in a cigarette users roll themselves.

speed: A drug that speeds up some of the brain's work.

For Further Exploration

Virginia Aronson, *How to Say No*. Philadelphia: Chelsea House, 2000. Good current information on the numbers of teens and preteens using drugs in the United States.

Bruce Brooks, *Woodsie, Again*. New York: Laura Geringer Books, 1999. A story of a young hockey team with players who are using marijuana.

Rhoda McFarland, *Cocaine*. New York: Rosen Publishing, 1997. Although somewhat challenging in its reading level, this book has a good chapter on why teens use drugs.

Suzanne Murdico, *Drug Abuse*. Austin, TX: Raintree Steck-Vaughn, 1998. Good section on drugs and the law.

Stanley Williams, *Gangs and Drugs*. New York: PowerKids Press, 1996. A former gang leader now in prison tells about the dangers of getting involved with drug dealing and its violence.

Index

Picture Credits

About the Author

Gail B. Stewart has written over ninety books for young people, including a series for Lucent Books called The Other America. She has written many books on historical topics such as World War I and the Warsaw ghetto.

Stewart received her undergraduate degree from Gustavus Adolphus College in St. Peter, Minnesota. She did her graduate work in English, linguistics, and curriculum study at the College of St. Thomas and the University of Minnesota. She taught English and reading for more than ten years. Stewart and her husband live in Minneapolis with their three sons.